PEOPLE & PLACES

Germany

E02889

A TEMPLAR BOOK

First published in Great Britain in 1989
by Macmillan Children's Books
A division of Macmillan Publishers Ltd
4 Little Essex Street
London WC2R 3LF and Basingstoke

Devised and produced by Templar Publishing Ltd
107 High Street, Dorking, Surrey RH4 1QA

Series Editor Sue Seddon
Designer Robert Mathias, Publishing Workshop
Photo-researcher Hugh Olliff

Colour separations by Positive Colour Ltd, Maldon, Essex
Printed by L.E.G.O., Vicenza, Italy

British Library Cataloguing in Publication Data
Phillpotts, Beatrice
    Germany
    1. Germany
    I. Title.   II. Series
    943.087'8

ISBN 0 333 46609 8

Contents

A NATION DIVIDED

Germany, once a single nation, was divided into two separate countries after World War 2. The Eastern part is called the German Democratic Republic and the Western part is called the Federal Republic of Germany. They are more simply known as East Germany and West Germany.

There is a tightly guarded border between East and West Germany. It was erected by East Germany from 1952 onwards to protect its style of government. East Germany has a communist government while West Germany has a western-style democracy. The two countries think very differently about the way in which nations should be governed.

West Germany is a leading member of the group of Western European countries that belong to the European Community (EC). East Germany is an important member of the group of countries and trading partners in Eastern Europe, known as the Eastern Bloc. Although both countries do most of their business quite separately, they have kept a special trade link with each other. They share the same language and culture, and many German families have relatives and friends in both East and West Germany.

Symbol of East Germany
The Brandenburg Gate in East Berlin is a ceremonial archway, built in 1789. It was turned round to face east when Berlin was divided. It now stands as a symbol of modernized East Berlin.

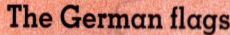

The German flags

The black, red and gold of the West German flag dates back to the colours worn by the Prussian army at a historic victory over Napoleon in 1813.

The East German flag adds a hammer, a wreath of grain and dividers to represent the union of industry, agriculture and the sciences.

Symbol of West Germany
The steep, rocky banks of the River Rhine are dotted with medieval castles. Some of these were owned by robber-knights who stole from boats travelling down the Rhine. They are now a popular tourist attraction.

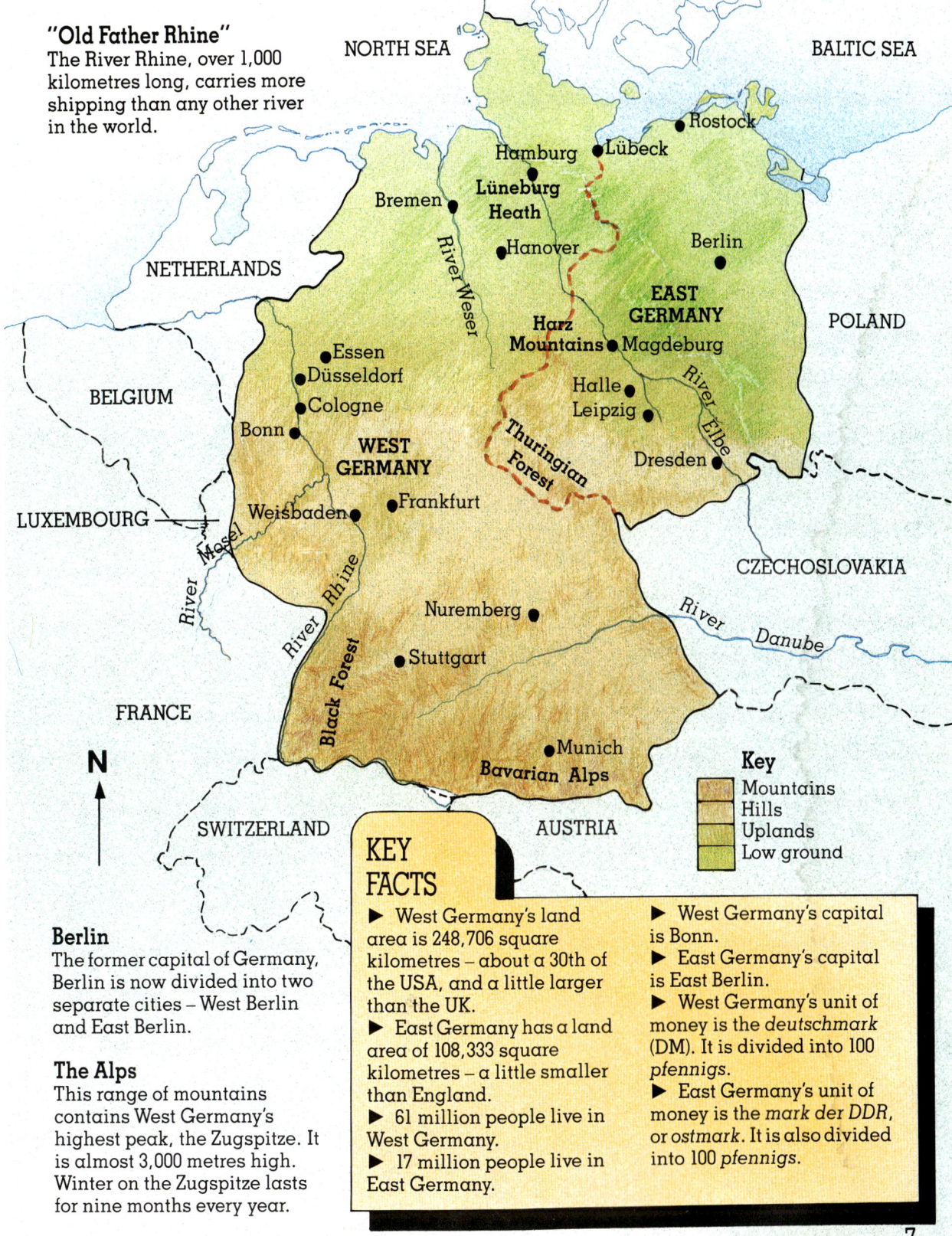

"Old Father Rhine"
The River Rhine, over 1,000 kilometres long, carries more shipping than any other river in the world.

NORTH SEA

BALTIC SEA

• Rostock

Hamburg • Lübeck

Lüneburg
Heath

Bremen •

Hanover •

Berlin •

NETHERLANDS

River Weser

**EAST
GERMANY**

POLAND

Essen •
Düsseldorf •
Cologne •

Harz
Mountains

Magdeburg •

Halle •
Leipzig •

River Elbe

Bonn •

BELGIUM

**WEST
GERMANY**

Thuringian
Forest

Dresden •

Weisbaden •
Frankfurt •

River Rhine

LUXEMBOURG

River Mosel

CZECHOSLOVAKIA

Nuremberg •

River Danube

Black Forest

Stuttgart •

FRANCE

Munich •
Bavarian Alps

Key
Mountains
Hills
Uplands
Low ground

N ↑

SWITZERLAND

AUSTRIA

Berlin
The former capital of Germany, Berlin is now divided into two separate cities – West Berlin and East Berlin.

The Alps
This range of mountains contains West Germany's highest peak, the Zugspitze. It is almost 3,000 metres high. Winter on the Zugspitze lasts for nine months every year.

**KEY
FACTS**

► West Germany's land area is 248,706 square kilometres – about a 30th of the USA, and a little larger than the UK.
► East Germany has a land area of 108,333 square kilometres – a little smaller than England.
► 61 million people live in West Germany.
► 17 million people live in East Germany.

► West Germany's capital is Bonn.
► East Germany's capital is East Berlin.
► West Germany's unit of money is the *deutschmark* (DM). It is divided into 100 *pfennigs*.
► East Germany's unit of money is the *mark der DDR*, or *ostmark*. It is also divided into 100 *pfennigs*.

ICH BIN DEUTSCH

German is an important language. As well as being spoken in East and West Germany, it is the official language of Austria and Liechtenstein and is spoken in Switzerland and parts of Belgium and France. More than 100 million people speak German as their first language and every tenth book in the world is published in German.

Germany was originally made up of different tribes, who each had their own language and customs. The German language spoken today is a mixture of these original tribal languages, or dialects. Some Germans still speak their local dialects as well as standard German, and people from different regions do not always understand each others' dialects.

Some Germans have moved away from their traditional homes in search of work in cities. Many moved from East to West Germany before, during and after the division of the country. Work opportunities in West Germany have also attracted people from other countries, such as Italy and Turkey, who have brought their own customs and languages with them. All these movements have made the traditional regional differences of language and customs much less distinct than they were at the beginning of this century.

X-ray vision
Wilhelm Konrad von Röntgen discovered X-rays when he experimented with electricity. In 1898 he took the first X-ray picture – of his wife's hand. He was awarded the Nobel prize in 1901 for his discovery.

Famous German Firsts

Time and space
Albert Einstein gave scientists new ideas about time and space. He won the Nobel prize in 1921 for his revolutionary suggestion that light might be a stream of tiny particles.

Print revolution

Johannes Gutenberg was the first printer to make type which could be taken apart and used again. Gutenberg's Bible, produced in 1455, was the first printed work to use this revolutionary process.

Driving ambition

Karl Benz built the first successful petrol-driven car in 1885. It was a three-wheeled vehicle. In 1886 Gottlieb Daimler produced the first successful four-wheeled petrol-driven car. Here Daimler is driven in the car.

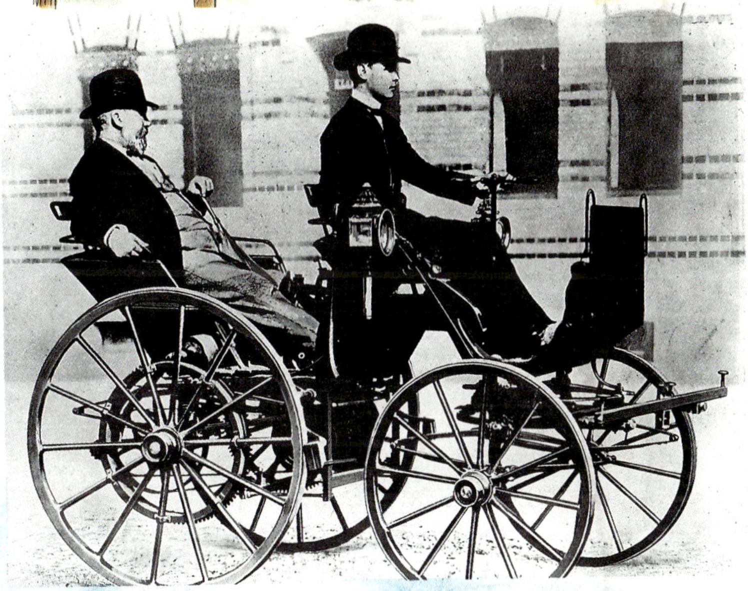

Flights of fancy?

In 1900 Count Ferdinand von Zeppelin built the first airship that could be steered.

MOUNTAINS AND FORESTS

Thousands of years ago, Germany was covered in thick forests of oak, birch and beech. Much of this woodland has since been cleared to make way for cities, factories and farms, but more than a quarter of Germany is still forested, much of it with pine trees.

Some of the most spectacular wooded areas are in mountainous areas, such as the Black Forest, in West Germany. The romantic image of East and West Germany is that both are all mountains and forests, but in fact, the landscape is very varied. There are plains in the north – a wide belt of low-lying heath and marsh, dotted with shallow lakes. Further south, the land rises abruptly in a series of heavily wooded mountain chains, divided by broad, fertile valleys. In the extreme south of West Germany, forests give way to flowery mountain meadows and then the snowy peaks of the Alps. Germany's richly varied landscape attracts many tourists.

East and West Germany have a temperate, generally mild climate, with a well-distributed, fairly heavy rainfall. East Germany and parts of West Germany, particularly the south and east, have plenty of snow in winter.

KEY FACTS

▶ Vast areas of the forests of Erzgebirge, in East Germany, have been destroyed by industrial pollution. The state is taking urgent measures to reduce it.

▶ The growing season for crops, from the last frost in spring to the first frost in autumn, varies only slightly across the two countries, averaging 212 days in Wiesbaden, central West Germany, and 205 days in Berlin, central East Germany.

▶ Wiesbaden, in West Germany, is famous for its hot, salt-water springs. The most powerful produces 500,000 litres daily at 65.7°C.

▶ Average temperatures in Munich range from –2°C in winter to 17°C in summer. In East Berlin temperatures vary from 0.5°C in winter to 19°C in summer.

Jingle bells, jingle bells...
Sleigh rides through the winter landscape of the Thuringian Forest in East Germany, are popular. The Vesser Valley, East Germany's most important nature reserve, lies in the Thuringian Forest.

Historic heathland

Lüneburg Heath (right), in the north of West Germany, has remained unchanged through many centuries. It covers 200 square kilometres and it has become well-known for a special breed of sheep, called *Heidschnucken*.

Mountain retreat

Surrounded by the forests and mountains of the Bavarian Alps, Neuschwanstein Castle could have come straight out of one of the fairy stories written by the brothers Grimm. In fact, it was built by Ludwig II of Bavaria in the 1870s.

COUNTRYSIDE AND CONSERVATION

Every third person in West Germany lives in a town or city. In East Germany, the figure is even higher – two out of three people are city dwellers. This means that large areas of German countryside – particularly the mountain forests – are almost uninhabited, and a great variety of wildlife still lives there. Some of the rarest animals in the region include the lynx of the cat family, which has been seen near the Czechoslovakian border, and the wildcat, from the Harz Mountains. The golden eagle was almost extinct, but it has begun to breed again in the Alpine districts of West Germany.

East and West Germany have created many nature reserves, where wildlife is protected. Industrial pollution, such as acid rain, is a threat to their forests and they are working together to control this and to conserve threatened species of plants and animals. West Germany now has a political party devoted to protecting the environment. Its members are called "The Greens" and the number of seats it has in the *Bundestag*, or Lower House of Parliament, almost doubled in the mid 1980s.

Rubbish power

West Germany uses some types of domestic rubbish as a useful source of energy. The rubbish is burned in special boilers and the energy given off is used to heat blocks of flats in some areas.

Saving the forests

Acid rain kills trees and has destroyed whole sections of forest in Germany. Both governments are trying to reduce the amounts of harmful sulphur dioxide gas in the air, which, when mixed with rain drops, falls as acid rain. Power stations, chemical plants and car exhausts all give off sulphur dioxide. Some species of pine trees are more resistant to this form of pollution, such as types of Swiss spruce, and these can be planted in high-risk areas.

The survivors

Not all Germany's animals are in danger of extinction. Wild boar (right), adders and deer live in woodland. Chamois, a type of deer, and ibex, a type of goat, live in Alpine areas. There are also many hundreds of species of birds, plants and insects.

Eagle owl

Under threat

The animals and plants shown here are rare or threatened. They are specially protected in Germany.

White-tailed eagle

Horseshoe bat

Pheasant's eye

Wildcat

Elbe beaver

13

WORKING THE LAND

Many more people work in industry than in agriculture in both West and East Germany. Most of the farms in West Germany are fairly small and many of the farmers only work on their land part time. However, factory-style farms are on the increase, where machines have taken over much of the work so that one farmer can now produce more food. The main food crops – as in East Germany – are cereals, potatoes and sugar beet. Some of the most successful "factory" farms raise pigs and poultry. West German farmers have benefited from the formation of the EC, which has helped to fix fairer prices for their produce.

In East Germany, most of the farms are large co-operatives. This means that workers share the land, machines and animals and they are paid by the co-operative according to the number of days they have worked and the amount of money their farm has earned. Other farms are owned by the state. The government pays the workers on such farms. Many farming families have small plots of their own land, too, and the government fixes a fair price for their produce. Modern machines have made co-operative farming much more efficient.

KEY FACTS

▶ Ten East Germans in every 100 work in agriculture, and 9 of those 10 have trained for their job.
▶ Five West Germans in every 100 work in agriculture – in 1950, it was 20 in every 100.
▶ All the honey and almost half the eggs East Germans eat are supplied from the farm workers' own plots.
▶ West Germany is one of the biggest producers of timber in the EC – about one million trees are felled each year.
▶ East German grain production has doubled since 1950 and meat production is five times higher.

2,000 years of wine
Wine has been produced in West Germany since Roman times. It is famous for its white wines. The main wine producing areas are in the south-west along the River Rhine. Grapes are grown in vineyards on the slopes above the river. West Germany exports much of its wine, mainly to the UK and the USA.

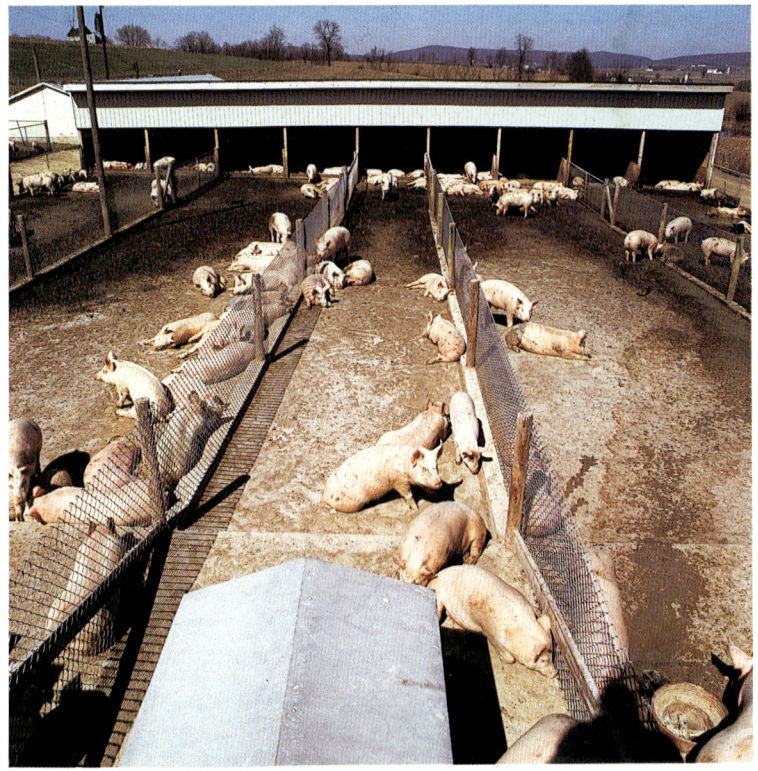

Fish fears

Over-fishing and pollution in the North Sea and the Baltic Sea have almost eliminated some of the most popular varieties of fish. East Germany and West Germany now control their fishing industries more tightly and they limit the numbers of fish caught each year.

Smoked bacon and sausages

Pork is a German speciality. It is eaten pickled, fried, roasted, boiled or baked. Pig rearing is one of the main farming industries. It has increased by a quarter in West Germany and by almost a half in East Germany. This is a pig-rearing farm in East Germany.

INDUSTRY AND POWER

The wealth of Germany is based mainly on industry. In East Germany, the industries are owned by the state, not by individual people, although there are some small privately owned businesses, such as garages and shops. East Germany is a member of the Council for Mutual Economic Assistance (Comecon) and it trades mostly with the USSR and the Eastern Bloc. In return, the USSR supplies it with oil and gas, but East Germany's main energy source is lignite, a type of coal, of which it is the world's third largest producer. East Germany is best known for its precision engineering, notably microscopes and camera lenses.

West Germany's industries are among the most successful in Western Europe and have brought the country a high standard of living. Its main trading partners in the EC are France and the Netherlands, and about half its exports go to the USA. West Germany's vast coal mines originally provided coal to power all its industries, but its stocks of coal are running out. Natural gas, imported oil and nuclear energy are now increasingly important power sources. West Germany is the third largest car manufacturer in the world. Volkswagen is one of the largest companies and it is planning to set up a big factory in East Germany.

Traditional crafts
German porcelain is admired throughout the world. Porcelain is made by firing (baking) articles made from clay and other substances at very high temperatures. Meissen, in East Germany, produces some of the best-known porcelain and it was there, in the early 18th century, that the secret of making hard-paste, or "true", porcelain was first discovered in the West.

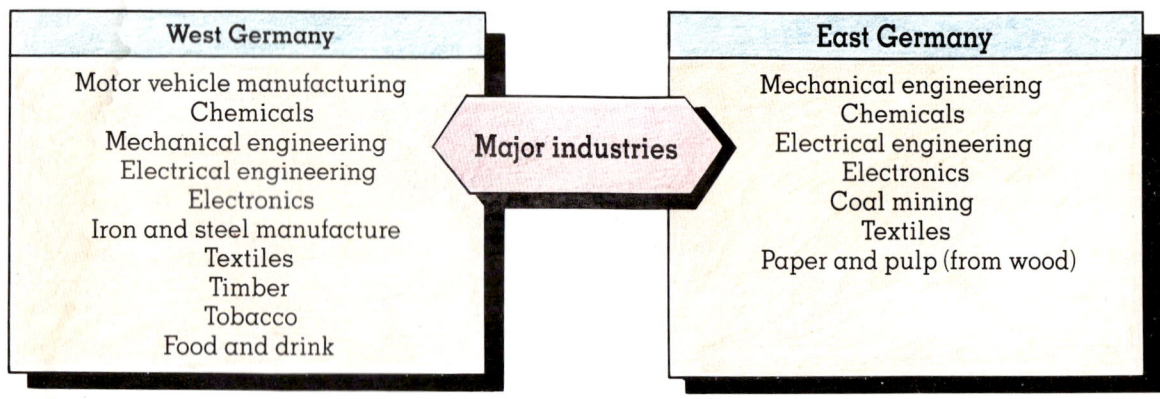

West Germany	Major industries	East Germany
Motor vehicle manufacturing Chemicals Mechanical engineering Electrical engineering Electronics Iron and steel manufacture Textiles Timber Tobacco Food and drink		Mechanical engineering Chemicals Electrical engineering Electronics Coal mining Textiles Paper and pulp (from wood)

Small is great

Micro electronics is one of the newest and fastest growing industries in East and West Germany. Many of the former coal-mining areas have switched to the micro electronics industry. Micro electronics are used in all sorts of modern machines, from big industrial robots to small digital watches. Here wafers of pure silicone from which micro chips are made are inspected in extremely clean surroundings.

The "Black Country"

The Ruhr (below), an area around the towns of Essen and Dortmund in West Germany, is the most heavily industrialized region in Europe. It is the centre of the West German iron and steel industry. Although there are many steel works and some coal mines in the area there are also woods and lakes.

FULL SPEED AHEAD

West Germany is a busy trading country and it has built up a very effective transport network to ensure that imports and exports move as quickly as possible. Heavy goods can be transported most economically by water, so West Germany's extensive network of rivers, especially the Rhine, and canals is particularly important. The roads and railways are also vital. They have been almost totally rebuilt since Germany was divided in 1945 and they are now some of the most modern in Europe. The Germans invented the *autobahn* (motorway). West Germany has an extensive system. It is second in total length to that of the USA.

Railways are the most important method of transport in East Germany. Computers now operate the major switchboards and junctions, and large stretches of track have been electrified, but steam engines are still used in some rural areas.

Canals and rivers carry much of East Germany's goods. The busiest waterway system is the River Elbe-Mittelland Canal-Rhine link between East and West Germany. A railway ferry from Rügen Island to Latvia in the USSR speeds trade links between East Germany and the USSR.

The Mittelland Canal
Building this 322-kilometre canal was a great engineering feat. At Minden, this aqueduct was constructed to carry the canal over the River Weser.

Travelling by train
Special, high speed Trans-European Express trains (TEE) connect West Germany with many major western European cities. All the carriages are first class and have public telephones. The TEE does not have to stop at the Austrian and Italian borders and so takes less than seven hours to travel from Munich to Milan, in Italy.

Inland waterways

The River Rhine lies at the heart of West Germany's inland waterway system. It carries more shipping than any other river in the world. It is linked to many parts of the country and to East Germany by a network of canals. A major new canal is planned to join the Rhine with the River Danube making a vital route through to south-east Europe. Here the Rhine flows through Cologne.

Travel by air

Germany was one of the great pioneers of commercial flying between World Wars 1 and 2. West Germany's Lufthansa airline offered non-stop flights from Berlin to New York as early as 1938, and it is still one of the leading international carriers. Lufthansa even runs its own train service linking the major airports, the "Lufthansa Express".

GUTEN APPETIT!

Germany created the world's best-known sausage – the Frankfurter – and sausages are a great German speciality. Every region in West and East Germany has its own favourite way of making them. Many of the regions also brew their own local beers, some of which are popular in other countries, too. West Germany is well known throughout the world for its wide range of white wines.

East German families spend more than a quarter of their income on food. Some foodstuffs, such as meat and coffee, are expensive and many fruits and vegetables cannot be bought frozen and are only in the shops when they are in season. To help make sure that families eat properly, the government has ensured that they can get cheap meals at their places of work, schools or kindergartens.

West Germans spend a fifth of their family income on food. The shops are well stocked with goods from home and abroad, and food prices are generally not expensive for West Germans. Factories start work at 6 am and school begins at 8 am, so many West Germans have two breakfasts. They might have rolls, eggs and coffee before they leave for work in the morning, then stop for a drink and cold meal or cheese snack at about 10 am.

"Evening bread"

Abendbrot or "evening bread" is what Germans call their evening meal. The main, hot meal is usually eaten at midday in East and West Germany. Many Germans eat this at work so their evening meal is an important family time when everyone is home again. Bread, sausages, cheese and fruit are often eaten in the evening.

Beer gardens

Bavaria, in West Germany, is well known for its good local beers – and its beer gardens. Many families enjoy eating and drinking outside during long summer evenings. Bavarian beers are all brewed under a strict purity code established nearly five centuries ago. At the famous beer festival the *Oktoberfest*, shown here, about 4.5 million litres of beer are drunk in 16 days.

Coffee and cake

When not at work, West Germans enjoy meeting for a chat at a café. In the afternoon they traditionally have *Kaffee und Kuchen* (coffee and cake). They drink freshly ground coffee and eat their favourite cakes selected from a large, mouth-watering display.

Regional specialities

Eintopf, "a meal in a pot", is a popular midday meal in Berlin.
It is a thick lentil, or pea, soup with sausage.

Rollmops are salted herrings. They come from the North Sea coast.

Black Forest cherry cake has layers of chocolate, cream and cherries.

21

WORDS AND MUSIC

Germany has produced some of the world's greatest musicians and writers. They are remembered at big annual festivals held in their honour, such as West Germany's opera festival at Bayreuth for Richard Wagner and East Germany's festival at Halle for the composer Handel.

German writers have helped influence the way many people think. Johann Wolfgang von Goethe was an important late 18th century poet. In the 19th century Karl Marx put forward a revolutionary political idea to give workers more power, which is now known as Marxism. At the same time, Friedrich Nietzsche was writing about the need to improve society.

The governments of East and West Germany are both anxious to make sure that the arts continue to flourish. All East Germany's theatres and concert halls are owned by the state and financed from the state budget. There is also a cultural fund, which awards grants to promising new talent. In West Germany, money for the arts comes from public and private sources, but the government provides generous grants.

Heroes and heroines
Germany has a strong folk tradition. Jakob and Wilhelm Grimm collected folk stories from all over Germany and published them between 1812 and 1814. Their collection includes such favourites as *Snow White* (above) and *Hansel and Gretel.*

"Curtain walls"
Walter Gropius (1883-1969), the architect, revolutionized modern ways of building. By using a framework of steel girders, he was able to build much thinner walls, with plenty of glass. Walls like this are called "curtain" walls. This method is now used all over the world. Gropius was also the inspiration behind a style of architecture and design known as the Bauhaus movement.

Famous composers

These great composers were
all born in Germany.

Johann Sebastian Bach
(1685-1750)

George Frederick Handel
(1685-1759)

Ludwig van Beethoven
(1770-1827)

Richard Wagner
(1813-1883)

Karlheinz Stockhausen
(Born 1928)

Great German artists

Albrecht Dürer (1471-1528) was
one of the most important early
artists in northern Europe. He
is mainly remembered for his
engravings and woodcuts.
Here is his well known picture
of hands. More recently, Max
Ernst (1891-1976) was a leading
surrealist artist, who explored
the world of dreams and secret
longings in his paintings.

23

FROM ROMANS TO REFORMATION

Powerful tribes originally ruled the land that is now Germany. In the first century AD, they drove the Romans back south of the Rhine. When the Roman Empire crumbled in the 5th century AD, the Franks – the strongest of the German tribes – took control.

Charlemagne was the greatest king of the Franks. Around AD 800 he created a huge empire called the Holy Roman Empire. Through the centuries, the Roman Catholic Church became very powerful within the empire. Many Germans believed it had become greedy and worldly. In the early 16th century, a religious movement, known as the Reformation, was started to reform the Roman Catholic Church. It grew into a new religion, known as Protestantism.

The religious division between the Protestants and the Roman Catholics flared up into a major European war – the Thirty Years' War (1618-1648). It was fought between the emperor, Ferdinand II, backed by his Roman Catholic armies, against the Protestant German princes, backed at different times by the English, Dutch, Danes, Swedes and French. When peace finally came, the Holy Roman Empire was no longer the great power in Europe.

Martin Luther
A German monk and professor at the University of Wittenberg, Luther (1483-1546) led the Reformation movement. He criticized the Roman Catholic Church for selling pardons to people who had committed sins, and was expelled from it. Luther then preached the new religion of Protestantism, which gave individuals more freedom of thought.

Charlemagne
Charlemagne (AD 747-814) ruled over a vast empire that stretched from Northern Germany, through Italy and France, down to northern Spain. Charlemagne was a keen scholar and built up a great library of beautifully decorated manuscripts.

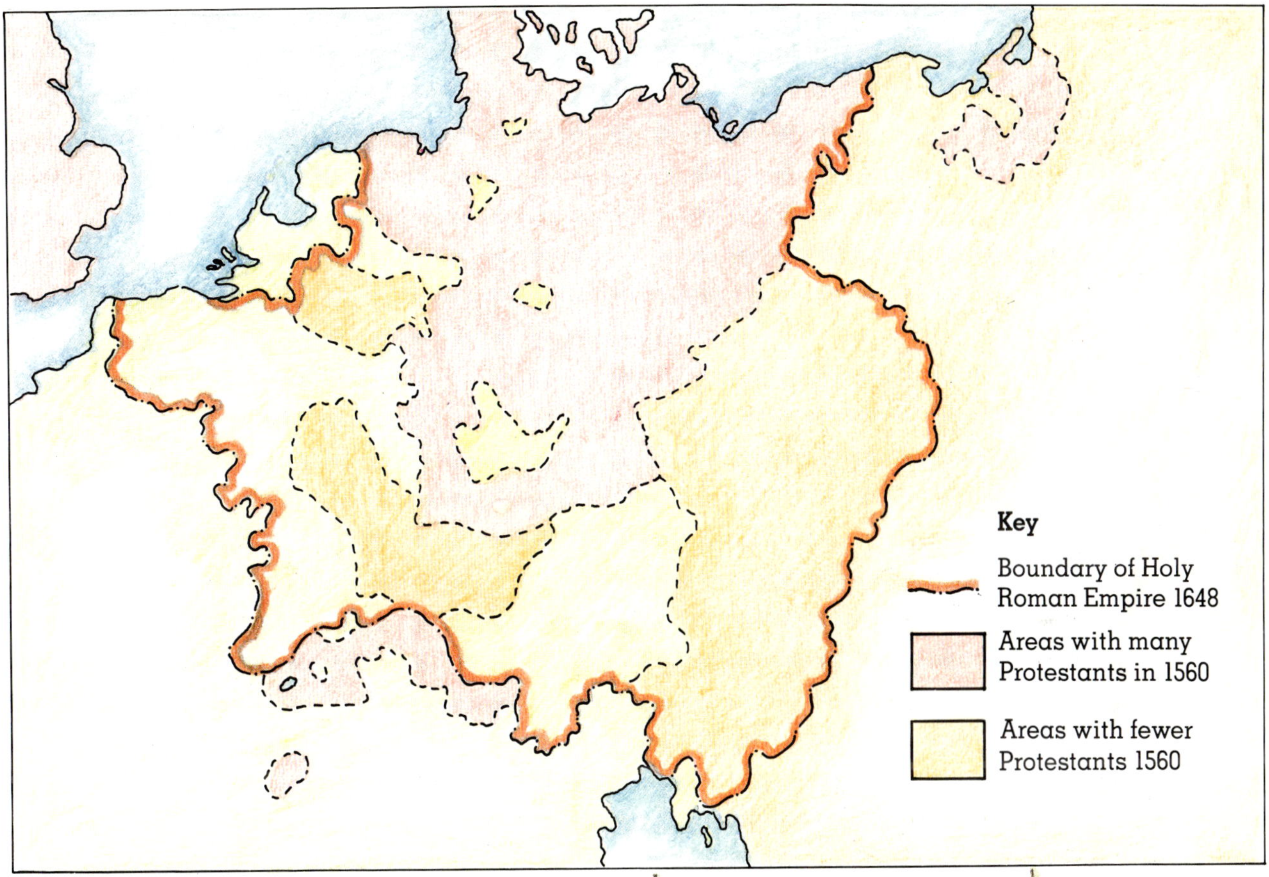
Key
Boundary of Holy Roman Empire 1648
Areas with many Protestants in 1560
Areas with fewer Protestants 1560

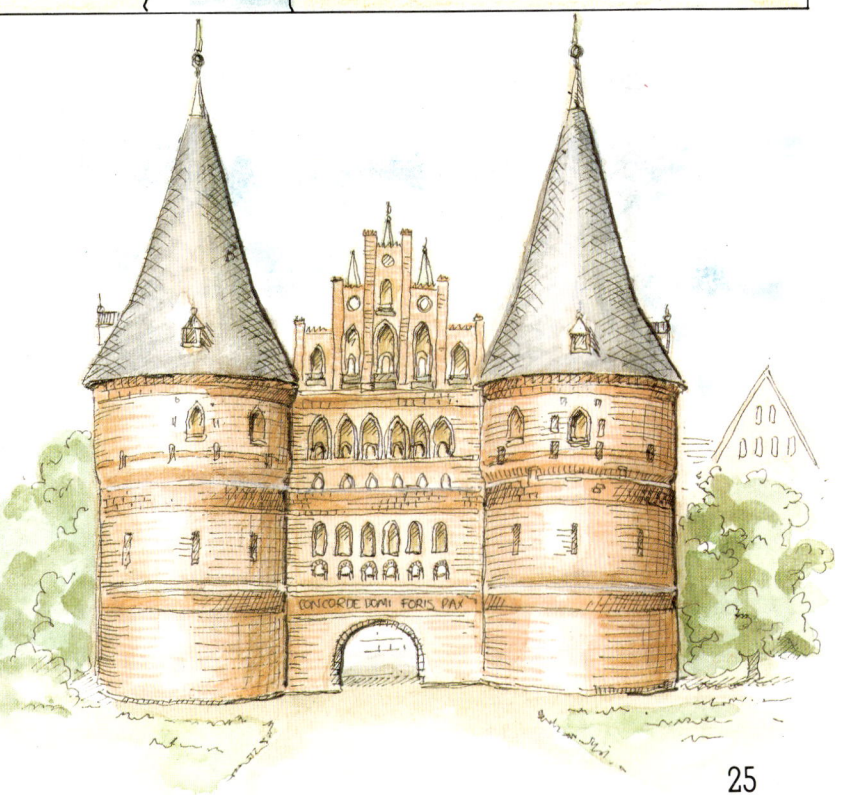

The German Reformation
This map of Germany during the Reformation (1517-1648), shows how widely Protestantism had spread.

CONCORDE DOMI FORIS PAX

Merchant power
In the 12th and 13th centuries German merchants returned from trips overseas with new, exotic spices, dyes and silks. Trade boomed and wealthy merchants and master craftsmen formed associations to protect their trading interests. The most powerful was the Hanseatic League. The money from trade helped finance splendid buildings, such as the fortified gateway at Lübeck.

THE RISE OF PRUSSIA

At the beginning of the 18th century, the Holy Roman or German Empire consisted of many small states governed locally by princes and nobility. The whole empire was ruled from distant Austria by the powerful Hapsburg family. During the 18th and 19th centuries Prussia, one of the states within the empire, became more powerful and struggled with Austria for power over the empire.

Frederick I, the "Soldier King", of Prussia turned Prussia into a strong military force. His son, Frederick the Great, fought and defeated the combined armies of Austria, France and Russia. When he died in 1786, Prussia was extremely powerful.

However, neither Prussia nor Austria was a match for Napoleon. The German Empire was invaded and occupied by France in the early 1800s. French rule was overthrown in 1814, and a German Confederation of 39 states under Austrian control was formed to replace the old empire.

More and more Germans wanted a united Germany. In 1866, Prussia forced the Austrians into the Seven Weeks' War and defeated them. A German Confederation was then formed which excluded Austria. Prussia showed her power again when she defeated France in the Franco-Prussian War (1870-1871). In 1871, Prussia's king, William I, was created emperor of the reshaped Germany.

The "Iron Chancellor"
Otto von Bismarck (1815-1898) was responsible for creating the new unified Germany under Prussia. He became Prime Minister in 1862 and Chancellor of the Empire in 1871. Bismarck believed that Prussia would achieve greatness only through "blood and iron" – war. He was responsible for Prussian victories over Denmark (1864), Austria (1866) and France (1870).

Maria Theresa
The Empress Maria Theresa (1717-1780) was a member of the powerful Austrian Hapsburg family. The Hapsburgs ruled the Holy Roman Empire from the 15th to the 19th century.

Maria Theresa fought a series of wars against Frederick the Great – the War of the Austrian Succession (1740-1748) and the Seven Years' War (1756-1763) – but she was unable to destroy Prussia.

A palace at Potsdam

Frederick the Great had a magnificent palace built at Potsdam near the Prussian capital, Berlin, in 1745. He admired the French and gave his palace a French name, "Sans Souci" (carefree). Frederick entertained many musicians, artists and writers at Sans Souci. The French philosopher, Voltaire, had his own set of rooms there.

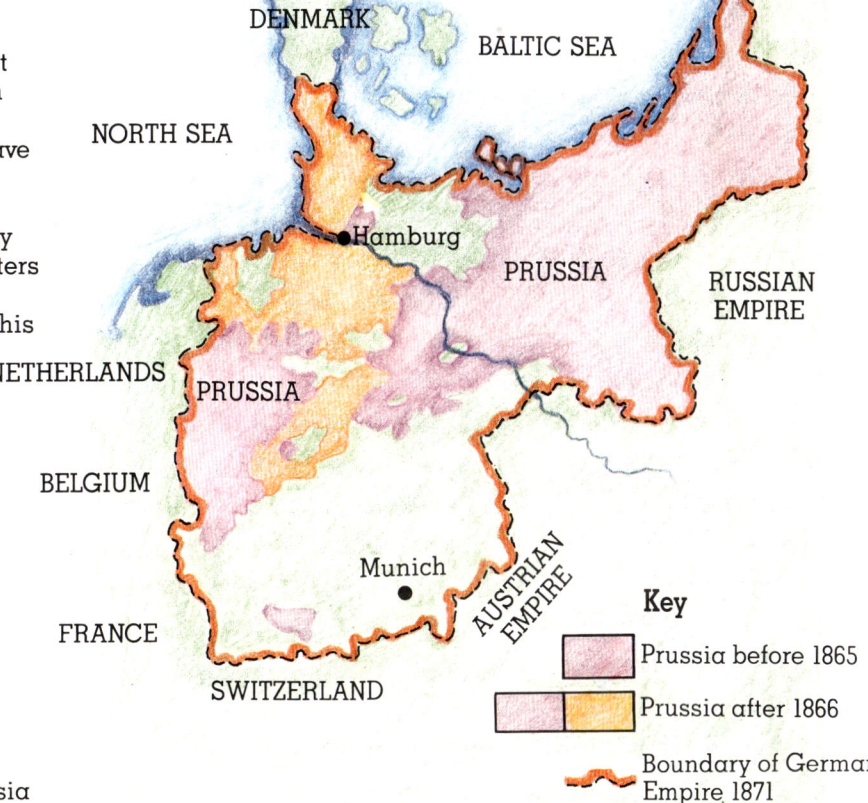

DENMARK

BALTIC SEA

NORTH SEA

•Hamburg

PRUSSIA

RUSSIAN EMPIRE

NETHERLANDS

PRUSSIA

BELGIUM

Munich

AUSTRIAN EMPIRE

FRANCE

SWITZERLAND

Key

Prussia before 1865

Prussia after 1866

Boundary of German Empire 1871

Prussian power

This map shows how Prussia grew in the 19th century.

WORLD AT WAR

In the first half of the 20th century, Germany fought and lost two world wars – and almost destroyed itself.

Germany's support for Austria against Russia started World War 1 in 1914. The combined might of the Allied Powers, which included Russia, France, the UK and the USA won the "Great War" in 1918, and a new German republic was created to replace the empire.

Germany lost a lot of money because of the war and the heavy compensation it had to pay the Allies. Six million were unemployed in 1933, when Adolf Hitler and his Nazi party were swept to power. Hitler built up the economy and established a powerful army. Then he set about conquering Europe.

In 1939, Hitler invaded Poland and started World War 2. Germany was successful at first but in 1941, the USA and the USSR joined Britain against Hitler. In 1945, Germany surrendered.

Trench warfare

World War 1 is remembered for its trench warfare, which forced soldiers to fight in the most horrifying conditions. When Germany failed to capture Paris in 1914, its armies dug a great line of trenches across Belgium and northern France from which to fight the Allies.

Mountains of money

By 1922, Germany's economy was in a terrible state. It cost so much money to buy even the simplest things, such as a loaf of bread, that cash registers in the shops became useless. This grocer is using a tea chest to hold all his shop's money.

Adolf Hitler

Hitler was born in Austria in 1889, but later moved to Germany. He joined the National Socialist, or Nazi, Party in 1919 and was elected its president in 1921. The Nazis believed that Germans should be a perfect, blond, blue-eyed race, superior to other people. This extreme belief led to the appalling ill-treatment and death of many millions of Jews, who were accused of not having "pure" German blood. It is thought that Hitler shot himself as the Russians advanced on Berlin in 1945.

The division of Germany

After Germany surrendered in 1945, the USSR, UK and USA met at the Potsdam Conference (right) to decide on Germany's future. The Allies could not agree on a style of government for the defeated country and divided it into four sectors controlled by the UK, USA, France and USSR. The USA, France and the UK united the three areas of Germany they occupied and the state of West Germany was formed on 15 September 1949. The USSR founded the communist state of East Germany on 7 October 1949.

THE TWO BERLINS

Berlin was in the middle of the Russian-controlled part of Germany at the end of World War 2. It was Germany's capital city, however, and the centre of communications, so each of the four Allies controlled a sector of it.

When Germany was divided into two states, Berlin was also divided. The Russian-controlled section became East Berlin, which the East Germans regard as their capital city. The section controlled by France, the UK and the USA became West Berlin. West Germany does not govern West Berlin but it has special links with the city, including the right to represent it to the outside world.

Free movement between East and West Germany was stopped by East Germany, when increasingly large numbers of East Germans who disagreed with the Russian-backed government crossed over to the West. Many of them were highly trained specialists such as scientists and doctors, who were vitally needed in East Germany. From 1952, the frontier was tightly guarded. In 1961, the East Germans built the Berlin Wall (below) to seal off East Berlin. The division of Germany – and its former capital – was now complete.

KEY FACTS

▶ The Berlin Wall was begun on 13 August 1961.
▶ It was built of concrete slabs topped with barbed wire. It had 209 watch towers, 131 bunkers, 108 kilometres of trenches and 272 kilometres of guard dog runs.
▶ 14,000 border guards originally patrolled it day and night.
▶ When the Wall reached houses and buildings, the doorways were simply blocked off.
▶ West Berlin became an artificial "island", ringed by 165 kilometres of concrete.
▶ The Wall divides many families and friends. The telephone now provides a vital link between people who were cut off from each other. Almost half the phone calls from West to East Germany are made from West to East Berlin.
▶ From 1961 to 1983, 72 people attempting to escape from East Berlin to West Berlin have been killed trying to cross the Wall.

Key

![Berlin Wall]	Berlin Wall
![Frontier]	Frontier
● ● ● ● ●	Division of sectors
![Waterways]	Waterways

Beating the blockade

In 1948, Russia quarrelled with the three Western Allies over a new money system for Berlin. As a result, the Russians blockaded the Allies' sectors of Berlin. For over 10 months there was no road or rail traffic and all vital supplies had to be flown in (above). There was strict rationing. Huge crowds cheered the first truck, when the blockade was lifted in 1949.

Berlin divided

The map shows the four sectors of Berlin originally controlled by the Allies. The Allies still maintain a special presence. They control air traffic over Berlin and their soldiers patrol the borders.

31

GERMANY NOW

West Germany has worked hard to rebuild its ruined industries since 1949. Its remarkably successful recovery is known as the "Economic Miracle".

Political power in West Germany is shared between the central government and the regional states (*Länder*). At present, five political parties are represented in parliament, covering a wide range of different views. West Germans take a keen interest in both national and local elections. More than 80 per cent of the population usually vote.

East Germany is now one of the most prosperous countries in Eastern Europe, although its standard of living is not as high as that of West Germany. Its economic recovery did not get going until the early 1960s, but progress has been rapid since then.

Close links are still maintained with the USSR. East Germany's political system is modelled on the Soviet Union, with the Communist Party of East Germany (known as the SED) responsible for all decision making. Young people aged between 14 and 25 belong to the communist Free German Youth organization. Religion continues to play an important role in East Germany, although it is a communist and therefore officially atheist (non-believing) state. Almost half the population are Protestants.

Taking the waters

Germany has many natural springs of hot or cold mineral water which can be good for the health. The Romans were the first to use the healing qualities of the springs. Over the centuries towns called spas grew up around the springs. Today, the spas offer modern medical treatments in addition to the traditional cures of bathing in or drinking the waters. Treatments at spas are very popular in East Germany.

Karl Marx Order

Glittering prizes

East Germany has two special awards for individuals or organizations who have made some outstanding contribution to the state. The Karl Marx Order is the highest award. The Star of International Friendship is awarded for international friendship and preserving peace.

Star of International Friendship

Health care

All East Germans, and West Germans on low incomes, belong to state health schemes which pay for their medical treatment. Many West Germans belong to private health schemes. Here a patient is checked for heart disease.

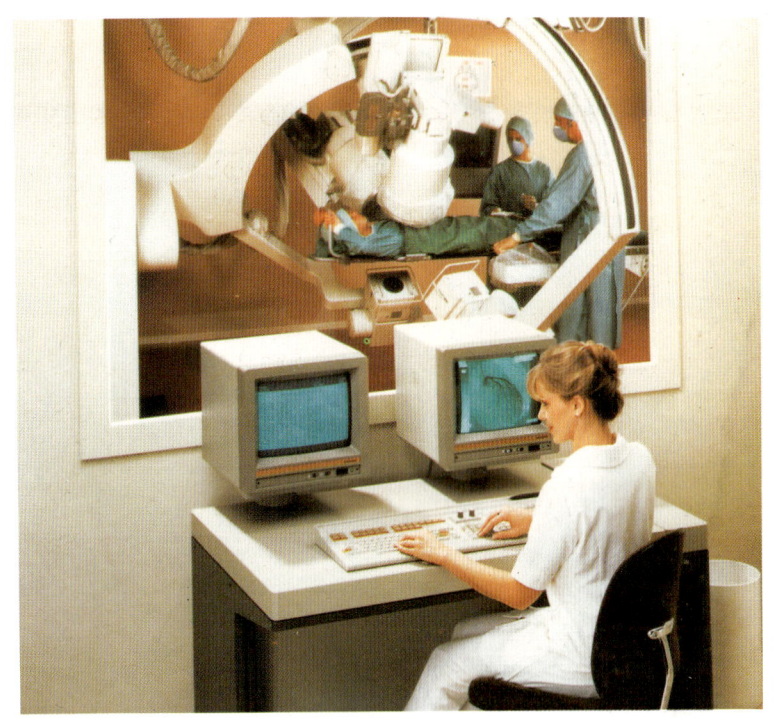

West Germany's state system
The Federal President is head of state, but the Chancellor, who is head of government, is more powerful.

Voters

Federal Council

Federal Parliament

Federal Cabinet

Federal Chancellor

Federal President

East Germany's state system
The Council of State is a collective, or group, head of state. The Council of Ministers is the collective government.

Village Assemblies

District Assemblies

County Assemblies

People's Chamber

Council of Ministers

Council of State

THE DAILY NEWS

The state owns and controls the main sources of communications in East Germany. The television network has two channels. It is linked by a television system called *Intervision* to the other Eastern Bloc countries. The feature films, documentaries and cartoons made by the state-owned film company, *DEFA*, are very popular. They are shown on television and in the cinema. The radio network is also government-owned and, like the newspapers, it is often used to give the government's point of view about many subjects.

West Germany prides itself on the freedom of its television, radio and press. There are two national television companies with three television channels – popularly known as One, Two and Three, between them. "One" and "Two" transmit programmes of national interest, while "Three" transmits programmes of local interest. There is one radio company (ARD) which broadcasts nationally and there is a wide choice of local radio stations.

Read all about it

Most East Germans read *Neues Deutschland*, the official SED daily newspaper. It is probably the best-known East German paper internationally. West Germany's best-selling daily paper is the *Bild Zeitung*. Magazines with stories about film and pop stars and the British royal family are popular in West Germany. Here daily newspapers are on sale in West Germany.

Dishing it up

Cable television is now available in West Germany for anyone who wishes to subscribe to it. Many households are also installing their own satellite dishes. These can directly pick up programmes beamed down into West Germany and neighbouring countries by different satellites. The choice of television channels has therefore grown enormously.

FAMILIES AND FESTIVALS

In the past, grandparents, parents and children usually lived together. Now it is more common for German children to leave home when they are adult, and family units have become smaller. Housing shortages are a problem because many people have moved from the country to the city in search of work. Most city dwellers live in rented flats.

Family ties are important. Sunday is often a family day, and a time to visit grandparents, or relatives. At Christmas and Easter, there are traditional family festivities, such as visiting the big Christmas fairs, or searching for hand-painted Easter eggs.

East Germans have about four weeks holiday a year – some workers, such as miners, get up to eight weeks. Travel outside the Eastern Bloc is not encouraged and most families go camping or caravanning by the sea, or in the mountain forests of East Germany.

West Germans have at least five weeks holiday. More than half the population travels abroad – Italy, Spain, Yugoslavia and Greece are popular destinations. West German families enjoy seaside and "activity" holidays.

Family flats

In Germany some estates of modern flats have a day nursery for the children of working mothers, a school and shops. Some flats have their own balcony gardens, where people can eat outside in the summer. In West Germany many flat dwellers have garden plots on the outskirts of the city where they can spend their leisure time.

Beside the seaside

The sandy beaches and islands of the North Sea and the Baltic attract many holidaymakers in the summer. Enormous wicker chairs dot the most popular beaches. They can be used as changing areas – and windbreaks as here in Sylt, West Germany.

Fun for all

East Germany's Day of the Republic festival is an important public holday. It is held every October to celebrate the founding of East Germany. All sorts of local activities are organized. In the cities, there are big torchlit processions.

AT THE MARKET

Most shops in East Germany are owned and run by the state. The choice of goods for sale can be small. However, as the economy improves, the choice is growing. Large new supermarkets have been built in town centres, such as East Berlin. These stores offer a wide range of goods. Some of the smaller shops are still privately owned, particularly those supplying special services, such as hairdressers or shoe repairers. The state subsidizes the cost of many goods, so the East Germans are protected from sharp price increases.

West Germany's shops are privately owned. They compete with each other to attract customers and the most popular stores offer the widest range of goods at the lowest prices. Small family-run "corner" shops often find it difficult to match the cheap prices charged by the big supermarkets, who make their profits by selling to greater numbers of shoppers. West Germans enjoy a high standard of living and the wide choice of goods for sale reflects the country's prosperity.

Home grown
Open-air markets are popular shopping places in both East and West Germany. They stock fresh produce from market gardens and allotments. Dried herbs are often sold as natural remedies for different kinds of illnesses.

No cars

Many West and East German towns feature specially designed pedestrian shopping precincts. In the centres of some old towns, cars have been banned and outdoor cafés have taken over the roads. More often, the pedestrian areas are new developments. They may be designed on several levels, with fountains and glass-covered walkways. This is a shopping precinct in Dresden, East Germany.

Shops for everyone

Some West German cities have areas where many foreign people live. There is a big Turkish population in West Berlin. Many shop signs are written in Turkish and German, and they stock Turkish as well as German goods.

TERM TIME

Eva lives in Hanover, in West Germany. She is nine years old and in her last year at primary school. She has to be up early because school starts at eight o'clock in the morning. At school she learns maths, sciences, German, history, geography, PE, religious studies, music and art. Classes finish soon after midday and Eva goes home for lunch. However, her school work is not over for the day – part of each afternoon is spent doing homework. Some schools also have classes on Saturday mornings.

Eva's cousin, Emil, lives in East Berlin. He is 12 years old and he goes to middle school. There are three levels at school – lower, middle and upper – but they are always in the same building, and Emil goes to the school nearest his home. In middle school Emil continues to study the subjects he began in lower school such as maths and German and he begins to study science, technology, sociology and his first foreign language – Russian. Like Eva, Emil starts school at eight o'clock and finishes at midday. Both his parents work, so he has lunch at school. Then he goes to the after-school club, where he can do his homework, or play sports with his friends until it's time to go home.

Choosing a school
East and West Germany have different school systems. In West Germany, parents and teachers decide which of the three types of secondary school a child should go to, when he or she leaves primary school. In East Germany, everyone receives the same education until 15 or 16. Then they decide which of two types of further school to attend.

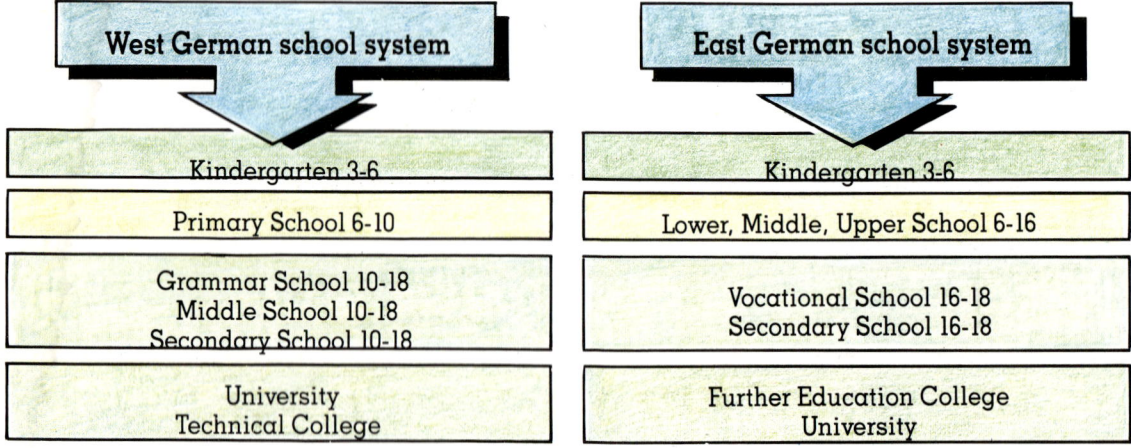

West German school system
Kindergarten 3-6
Primary School 6-10
Grammar School 10-18 Middle School 10-18 Secondary School 10-18
University Technical College

East German school system
Kindergarten 3-6
Lower, Middle, Upper School 6-16
Vocational School 16-18 Secondary School 16-18
Further Education College University

The "Blues" and the "Reds"

Many East German schoolchildren belong to the Pioneers youth movement, which is organized by the communist party. Pioneers organize special events locally and help with community work, such as looking after old people. They also attend large summer camps. Young Pioneers wear blue scarves. Senior members have red scarves.

Sweet cones

East and West German children traditionally take a big paper cone full of sweets to school on their first day at primary school.

Kindergartens

Kindergartens, or nursery schools, started in Germany. They are now common in many countries. Children can attend kindergarten from three to six years old. In West Germany, parents pay for their children to go to kindergarten. In East Germany, nursery schools are free.

GOING FOR THE GOLD

Sport is taken very seriously in East Germany. It is compulsory at school and pupils who show promise are encouraged to improve their skills. They can attend special schools, where classes are arranged around their training sessions. Sports stars are important members of society. They can get a place to live or a car more easily than most people and they are often given good teaching jobs when they stop competing. All this early training and encouragement has set a very high athletic standard. East Germany has won 445 Olympic medals since first entering the Games in 1956. It is a remarkable achievement. The top medal winners, USA and USSR, have won more but their countries are far larger.

The West Germans are also very keen on sport. One in every three people belongs to a sports club and there are more than 50,000 clubs in the country. Football is one of the most popular sports and the national team has done very well internationally. The state contributes to the cost of training its leading athletes and money also comes from private donors such as businesses. In 1972, the Olympic Games were held in Munich and West Germany won 13 gold medals.

Sport for the masses
Bicycling and walking are popular activities in West and East Germany. Special cycling and hiking routes have been created in the countryside.

Ice and snow
Germany has several important winter sports centres. Oberhof, in East Germany, attracts many skaters and skiers. It also holds competitions for ski jumping. Cross-country skiing is a major sport in West Germany. Thousands of enthusiasts meet for national runs in the Bavarian Alps.

Tennis champion
West Germany's Boris Becker (right) was the youngest player, at 17, to win the Wimbledon Tennis Championships in 1985. He also won there in 1986.

Record breakers

West Germany's Walter Röhrl is the only man to win two World Rally Drivers' Championships. He shares the record for four wins in the Monte Carlo Rally.

East Germany's Kornelia Ender won a record eight Olympic medals for swimming – four gold and four silver.

East Germany's Karin Kania has won a record four world titles for speed skating – and a record six overall titles at the World Sprint Championships.

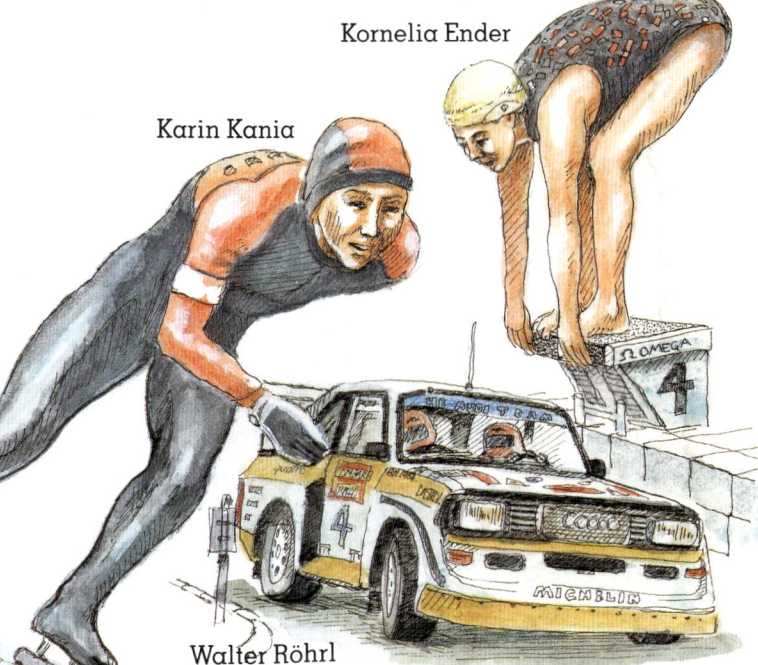

Kornelia Ender

Karin Kania

Walter Röhrl

LOOKING TO THE FUTURE

The closely guarded frontier that divides Germany into two separate states is part of the border known as the Iron Curtain that separates the Eastern Bloc from the West. It is also an important dividing line between the opposite styles of government in the East and the West. To keep a balance of power and protect their different viewpoints, East and West have formed separate military agreements. West Germany is a member of NATO, an alliance of Western Europe and the USA. East Germany is a member of the Warsaw Pact, which is a military alliance between six Eastern European states and the USSR. The border between East and West Germany, therefore, has a major international importance, and both NATO and the Warsaw Pact have built up a strong military presence along it.

Living on the "front line", West and East Germany are both keenly aware of the need for world peace. Despite the difficulties of living in a divided nation, each country is anxious to avoid any dangerous confrontations. Since signing the "good-neighbourly" treaty in 1972, the two states have worked to improve contacts between themselves. The new Soviet policy of *glasnost* – "openness" – may help raise the Iron Curtain even more.

Freedom of movement

East Germans wishing to visit relatives and friends in West Germany still face difficulties. Such visits are generally not approved, although during the mid-1980s more East Germans were allowed family visits to West Germany. East German pensioners are allowed to visit quite freely, however, and one and a half million take advantage of this every year. It is now much easier for West Germans to visit East Germany and many do. The border crossing shown on the right is in Berlin.

Planning for world peace

The historic agreement made between the USA and the USSR to reduce the numbers of nuclear missiles directly affects East and West Germany. It reverses the build-up of arms by NATO and the Warsaw Pact forces along the border. Here President Ronald Reagan of the USA shakes hands with the leader of the USSR, Mikhail Gorbachev. Future agreements may remove the need for such a powerful military presence.

Future hopes
Young people in West and East Germany are anxious to secure a peaceful future. They join all sorts of group activities to make their feelings public. This is an official Free German Youth party demonstration in East Berlin. The white crosses stand for East German opposition to NATO's nuclear weapons.

45

Index

Acknowledgements

Map illustration (page 6-7) by Ann Savage.
All other illustrations by Brian Hoskin except page 22: Paul
Bonner © Robert Mathias Publishing Workshop.
Photographic credits (a = above, b = below, m = middle, l = left,
r = right):
All cover pictures Zefa; page 9 Mercedes-Benz; page 11 a E Landschak/
Zefa, b R Jackson/German National Tourist Office; page 12
Greenpeace; page 13 Zefa; page 14 Adam/Zefa; page 15 G Heilman/
Zefa; page 17 a Siemens, b W Westerman/Zefa; page 18 Mueller/
Zefa; page 19 Damm/Zefa; page 20 Zefa; page 21 Damm/Zefa; page
22 Architectural Association; page 23 Bridgeman Art Library;
page 27 Hektor/Zefa; page 29 Robert Hut Library; page 30 Robert
Harding Picture Library; page 31 TRH Pictures; page 33 Siemens;
page 34 Goethe Institute; page 35 MBB-ERNO; page 36 Rust/Zefa;
page 37 Spectrum Colour Library; page 39 Hilmar/Zefa; page 41 a
Robert Harding Picture Library, b M Zur/Zefa; page 42 Adams
Picture Library; page 43 Sporting Pictures (UK) Ltd; page 44
Popperfoto/Reuter; page 45 Kappelmeyer/Zefa.